Arduino
Interrupts

Speed up your Arduino to be responsive to events

Claus Kühnel

Arduino Interrupts

Speed up your Arduino to be responsive to events

Claus Kühnel

ISBN-10: 3-907857-42-9

ISBN-13: 978-3-907857-42-7

www.ckskript.ch

The book and the circuits described procedures and programs, have been carefully created and tested. Nevertheless, errors and mistakes cannot be excluded.

Preface

Arduino family of microcontrollers has become an integral part of the world of electronics. Users of Arduino range from makers to enthusiasts to professionals. Therefore, it is not surprising that a large number of books on the different aspects of application and programming of Arduino are available.

This is not another book on these aspects. I would like to deal with interrupts, which make the execution of the Arduino program more effective.

Some years ago I published the book "Arduino: Hard- und Software Open Source Plattform" (ISBN 978-3-907857-16-8) in German language. From my readers I know that the section covering interrupts is seen as an important complement to the widely available basics. This was the base for writing this eBook which explains the usage of the interrupts of the ATmega328 based Arduino.

Knowledge of Arduino and its programming with the Arduino development environment (IDE) are assumed.

For the print edition all links were verified and changed if needed.

Claus Kühnel, in March 2019

Table of Content

1 Arduino Boards

If we talk about Arduino today we have to talk about the whole Arduino family. Starting with Arduinos based on Atmel's AVR microcontrollers now we have with Atmel's SAMD21 Cortex-M0 included in the family. Furthermore, with Arduino Yùn and Arduino Tian we have Arduinos enhanced by Linux devices.

Nevertheless, the ATmega328 based Arduino Uno Rev. 3 is the best-selling device of the Arduino family furthermore (Figure 1).

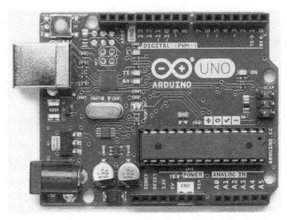

Figure 1   Arduino Uno Rev. 3

If you prefer a more compact solution then you will find Arduino Nano based on the same ATmega328 microcontroller as the Arduino Uno (Figure 2).

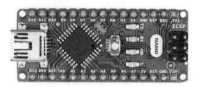

Figure 2   Arduino Nano

The assignment of the connectors of the Arduino Uno to the pins of the ATmega328 (and the alternative functions) is shown in the following tables:

I/O	0	1	2	3	4	5	6	7
	PD0	PD1	PD2	PD3	PD4	PD5	PD6	PD7
AVR	RxD	TxD	INT0	INT1	T0	T1	AIN0	SCK
				OC2B		OC0B	OC0A	

I/O	8	9	10	11	12	13
	PB0	PB1	PB2	PB3	PB4	PB5
AVR	ICP1	OC1A	OC1B	OC2A	MISO	SCK
			SS	MOSI		

Analog In	0	1	2	3	4	5
	PC0	PC1	PC2	PC3	PC4	PC5
AVR	ADC0	ADC1	ADC2	ADC3	ADC4	ADC5
					SDA	SCL

The complete pinout of both mentioned Arduinos is well documented by excellent diagrams which are too big and detailed for showing here. But, they can be downloaded from the following URLs.

For Arduino Uno use https://bit.ly/2CbUCUw and for Arduino Nano use https://bit.ly/2RIOwE0.

To read the specifications in detail you have to study the 662 pages of the ATmega328 data sheet (https://bit.ly/2RzKGcl). I tried to explain the functions used here so detailed that in normal case you do not need to read the data sheet for this exercises.

All programs are available for download on Github https://github.com/ckuehnel/ArduinoInterrupts.

2 Arduino ADC

Before I will come to interrupts some words to the internal Analog/Digital-Converter (ADC).

The ADC of ATmega328 is a complex module and therefore I will start using the ADC without interrupts first. The ADC offers various modes of operation not all supported by Arduino standard programming. Programming the ADC on register level offers further features.

2.1 Internal ADC and PWM as DAC

Arduino Uno has 6 analog inputs designated as ADC5 to ADC0. Figure 3 shows the block diagram of the ADC as a detail. For DAC we have to use a pulse-width modulated digital output.

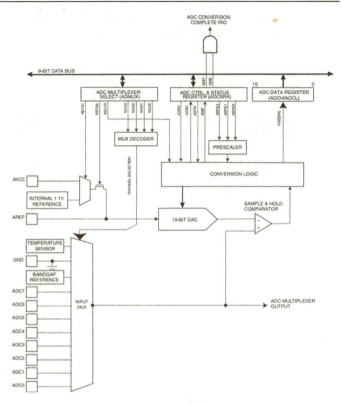

Figure 3   Block Diagram ATmega328 ADC

If less analog inputs are required, the analog inputs that are not required can also be used as GPIO (General Purpose I/O) or I^2C bus lines. The following table shows the multiple assignments of the Arduino connectors in this area. When used as digital IO, Analog In 0 - 5 correspond to I/O 14 - 19.

Analog In	0	1	2	3	4	5
I/O	14	15	16	17	18	19
AVR	PC0	PC1	PC2	PC3	PC4	PC5
	ADC0	ADC1	ADC2	ADC3	ADC4	ADC5
					SDA	SCL

Like all other pins, the analog inputs are also equipped with switchable pull-up resistors. However, a pull-up resistor that is switched on influences the AD conversion. Therefore, pull-up resistors must be disabled while the pin is configured as an analog input. Errors can also be expected if the connection has previously been configured as a digital output.

In the following program example, *adda.ino*, an output voltage is generated by PWM (pulse-width modulation). This voltage is smoothed to a DC voltage by a RC combination. This DC voltage is, in turn, supplied to the ADC, and the result of the AD conversion should then represent the value of the DA converter. Figure 4 shows the complete circuitry.

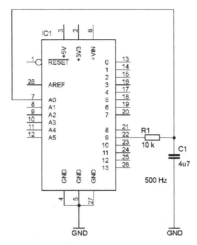

Figure 4   DA-AD-Conversion with internal Resources of Arduino

Arduino works with a PWM frequency of approximately 500 Hz. The RC combination (low-pass) should be dimensioned in practice according to the following formula:

14

$$\tau = R \cdot C = \frac{(10..1000)}{f_{PWM}}$$

If the time constant RC is selected too high, the settling time increases. If, on the other hand, it is too small, the filtering effect is too low.

The time constant of 47 ms chosen according to Figure 4 is rather at the lower end, which is why an optimal filter effect is not expected. But, this is sufficient to demonstrate the principle of DA-AD-conversion.

In the program example *adda.ino* (Listing 1), a PWM value is set to I/O9 with `analogWrite(AOUT, i)`. The low-pass filter output is connected to the analog input AIN0 of the internal ADC (ADC0). After a waiting time of 1 sec (`delay (1000)`) the result of AD conversion is read with `analogRead(AIN0)`. This procedure is repeated in an endless loop. The remaining instructions are for serial output and configuration only.

A special feature is still to be considered. The 8-bit Timer1 is used for the PWM, which is why only values between 0 and 255 can be set here. The internal ADC, however, has a resolution of 10 bits, which is why the results are between 0 and 1024. The factor 4 is therefore taken into account when calculating the deviation (ADC-4DAC).

```
// Title      : ADDA
// Author     : Claus Kuehnel <ckuehnel@gmx.ch>
// Date       : 2017-05-10
// Id         : adda.ino
// Tested w/  : Arduino 1.8.0
//
// DISCLAIMER:
// The author is in no way responsible for any problems
or damage caused by
// using this code. Use at your own risk.
//
// LICENSE:
// This code is distributed under the GNU Public License
```

```
// which can be found at
http://www.gnu.org/licenses/gpl.txt
//

const int AOUT = 9; // IO9 is PWM output
const int AIN0 = 0; // AIN0 is analog input

void setup()
{
  pinMode(AOUT, OUTPUT); // configure PWM output
  Serial.begin(19200); // baud rate of console output
  Serial.println("DAC\tADC\tADC-4DAC");
}

void loop()
{
  int i, val;
  for (i=0; i<256; i+=16)
  {
    analogWrite(AOUT, i); // set PWM value from 0 to 255
    delay(1000);
    Serial.print(i); // console output of DAC (PWM) value
    Serial.print("\t");
    val = analogRead(AIN0); // read ADC result
    Serial.print(val); // console output of ADC result
    Serial.print("\t");
    Serial.println(val - 4*i); // calculate deviation and
output it
  }
}
```

Listing 1   Source code *adda.ino*

After the start of the program *adda.ino* the console output can be viewed in the monitor of the Arduino IDE. Figure 5 shows the serial output of the individual conversions. The third column shows the calculated deviation ADC-4DAC which cannot show typical values for the internal ADC because of the non-optimum RC filtering.

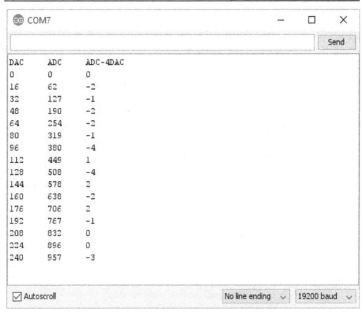

Figure 5   Console output of *adda.ino*

2.2 Internal ADC in Free Running Mode

The internal ADC of the Arduino can operate not only in the single conversion mode used by `analogRead()` but also in the free running mode. For the initialization of the free running mode and to readout the results of the AD conversion, however, one must use the direct register access.

The multiple registers are responsible for the operation of the ADC. At this point, only the initialization can be considered. To look for all options, you have to study the large-scale data sheet of the ATmega328.

	7	6	5	4	3	2	1	0
ADCSRA	ADEN	ADSC	ADATE	ADIF	ADIE	ADPS2	ADPS1	ADPS0

By register ADCSRA the ADC will be enabled (ADEN), the first AD conversion will be started (ADSC), and the Auto-trigger enabled (ADATE), required for free running mode. The bits ADPS2-ADPS0 select the prescaler for the ADC clock.

In order to achieve a maximum resolution of the AD converter, the internal circuit should be operated with an ADC clock between 50 and 200 kHz. If the prescaler bits are all set, an ADC clock of 125 kHz is set from the 16 MHz system clock by a divider of 128.

From the timing diagram in Figure 6 it can be seen that the AD conversion is completed after 13 clock cycles and a conversion time of approx. 100 µs is achieved with this prescaler.

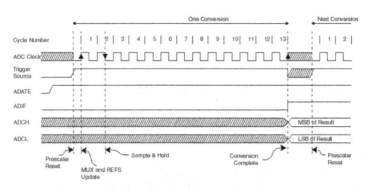

Figure 6   Timing Diagram Free Running Mode

	7	6	5	4	3	2	1	0
ADMUX	REFS1	REFS0	ADLAR	-	MUX3	MUX2	MUX1	MUX0

The analog reference voltage can be selected via the ADMUX register (REFS1, REFS0). I use AVcc = 5 V as reference voltage. The data format can be set to left or right justified (ADLAR) and the analog multiplexer is set via the bits MUX3-MUX0.

As can be seen from Figure 3, the analog inputs are not limited to the inputs ADC5-ADC0. Still interesting for commissioning are the internal bandgap reference, the internal ground and the temperature sensor. These are also queried as known input voltages in the program example.

The setup of the two registers can be found most easily from the source code of the program sample *free_running_adc.ino* (Listing 2).

```
// Title      : Free Running ADC
// Author     : Claus Kuehnel <ckuehnel@gmx.ch>
// Date       : 2017-05-10
// Id         : free_running_adc.ino
// Tested w/  : Arduino 1.8.0
//
// DISCLAIMER:
// The author is in no way responsible for any problems
or damage caused by
// using this code. Use at your own risk.
//
// LICENSE:
// This code is distributed under the GNU Public License
// which can be found at
http://www.gnu.org/licenses/gpl.txt

#define ADC4 0x44
#define ADC5 0x45
#define TEMPERATURE 0x48
#define BANDGAP 0x4E
#define GND 0x4F

// ADCSRA
#define FREE_RUNNING_MODE ((1<<ADEN) | (1<<ADSC) |
(1<<ADATE) | (1<<ADPS2) | (1<<ADPS1) | (1<<ADPS0))

#define PURPOSE "Test of Free Running ADC"

const byte LED = 13;

word adc_value;

void setADC(byte config)
```

```
{
  ADCSRA &= ~(1<<ADEN); // ADC disabled
  ADMUX = config;        // MUX selection
  ADCSRA = FREE_RUNNING_MODE; // start ADC
}

word getADC(void)
{
  return (ADCL | (ADCH << 8));
}

void printResult(void)
{
  digitalWrite(LED, 1); // LED on
  delay(10);
  adc_value = getADC();
  digitalWrite(LED, 0); // LED off
  Serial.print(adc_value, HEX); // output ADC value
  Serial.print("\t");
  Serial.print((float) adc_value*5./1024); // calculate
voltage and output
  Serial.println(" V\n");
}

void setup()
{
  pinMode(LED, OUTPUT);
  Serial.begin(19200);
  Serial.println(PURPOSE);
}

void loop()
{
  Serial.println("Bandgap Reference");
  setADC(BANDGAP);
  printResult();
  delay(1000);
  Serial.println("GND");
  setADC(GND);
  printResult();
  delay(1000);
  Serial.println("Temperature");
  setADC(TEMPERATURE);
  printResult();
  delay(1000);
}
```

Listing 2   Source code *free_running_adc.ino*

The initializations of the ADC registers are held in a series of `#define`s.

The `setADC()` function is used to configure the analog multiplexer. Before the multiplexer is set or changed, the ADC must be disabled. After configuration, the ADC is then enabled again and the first AD conversion can be started. After this start, the ADC runs in the Free Running Mode. This means, after each AD conversion, the result of the conversion is written to the registers ADCH and ADCL and a new conversion is started. The two registers can be read in the order ADCL followed by ADCH, as done in the function `getADC()`.

In the main loop of the program the inputs Bandgap Reference, Ground (GND) and Temperature Sensor are selected one after the other and converted. The result of the AD conversion is output in the function `printResult()`. Figure 7 shows the outputs of the program example.

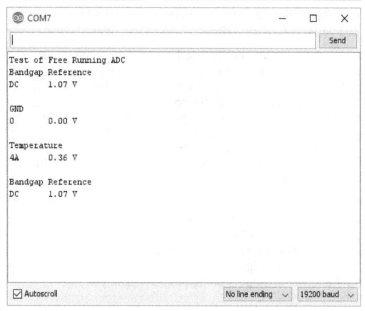

Figure 7   Terminal output *free_running_adc.ino*

3 Arduino Interrupts

In this chapter, the interrupt-controlled program flow is to be considered; which allows a direct response to external events.

Especially when measuring, and/or controlling processes, the reaction is required in specific time limits. Frequently the term "real-time capability" is used.

In computing, an interrupt is the interruption of a running program in order to execute a different, usually time-critical program, triggered by a specific event.

The triggering event is called interrupt request (IRQ). Thereafter, the Interrupt Service Routine (ISR) is executed. The execution of the original program is then continued after the interruption point (by a return from interrupt RETI).

The interrupt-controlled program flow is shown in Figure 8. The left branch is the conventional program sequence.

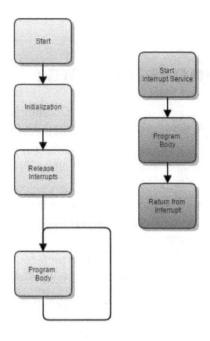

Figure 8 Interrupt controlled program flow

After the program has been started, the initialization of memory areas, variables and peripherals takes place. Subsequently, when used, the used interrupts are enabled. After these initialization steps, the program enters an endless loop.

If interrupts were enabled, the corresponding event can request an interrupt and the corresponding interrupt service routine (ISR) will be started. The execution of the interrupt service routine is terminated by a "return from interrupt" (reti) and the program processing continues after the interrupt point.

Interrupt service routines should be kept short in order to limit the interruption of the main program to the necessary minimum. If several interrupts are used, interrupt requests can be lost by long interruptions of the main loop.

Today, modern microcontrollers usually have powerful interrupt systems. We will look at selected aspects of the interrupt system of the ATmega328 used in Arduino Uno.

3.1 Contact to the outside world

When considering the interrupt behavior, the pins of the microcontroller used must be directly included. It is essential to consult the data sheet of the microcontroller used. The pin names of the Arduino Uno board do not help here. Figure 9 shows the ATmega328 pins on the Arduino Uno.

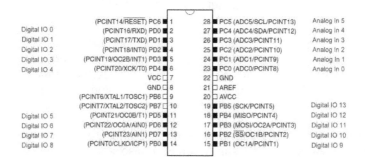

Figure 9   Naming of ATmega328 Pins vs. Arduino Uno

3.2 ATmega328 Interrupt System

Atmel's AVR microcontrollers can handle a variety of different interrupts. These interrupts and the reset have a so-called interrupt vector in the program memory. Each interrupt can be released individually.

The interrupt vectors are arranged in the form of a table at the lower end of the program memory. The priority of the respective interrupt is linked to the position in this table. The lower the address of the interrupt vector, the higher the priority.

If an interrupt is requested, the Global Interrupt Enable Bit is reset and all (further) interrupts are disabled. The application program can remove this lock. This lock is automatically released when the interrupt service routine (ISR) is excited by a "Return from Interrupt" (reti).

There are basically two different types of interrupts. The first type is triggered by an event which sets the relevant interrupt flag. The program counter is loaded with the address of the respective interrupt vector and the associated interrupt service routine is executed. If an interrupt request occurs, if the relevant interrupt is not enabled, then this interrupt request is saved and then processed only after the interrupt has been enabled. The same behavior also applies to the global interrupt.

The second type triggers only as long as the condition for the interrupt exists. If such a condition is terminated before the interrupt enable, then this interrupt is lost.

When the AVR microcontroller has completed an ISR, the program processing continues after the interruption point.

The status register is not automatically backed up so that this operation must be performed manually.

3.3 ATmega328 Interrupt Vector Table

Table 1 shows the interrupt vector table for the ATmega328.

The Arduino project uses the free C compiler AVR-GCC from the GNU Compiler Collection. For this reason, the vector names of the AVR-GCC for the ATmega328 are listed in the column to the right.

Vector No.	Program Address	Source	Interrupt Definition	AVR GCC Vector Name
1	0x00	RESET	External Pin, Power-on Reset, Brown-out Reset and Watchdog System Reset	
2	0x02	INT0	External Interrupt Request 0	INT0_vect
3	0x04	INT1	External Interrupt Request 1	INT1_vect
4	0x06	PCINT0	Pin Change Interrupt Request 0	PCINT0_vect
5	0x08	PCINT1	Pin Change Interrupt Request 1	PCINT1_vect
6	0x0A	PCINT2	Pin Change Interrupt Request 2	PCINT2_vect
7	0x0C	WDT	Watchdog Time-out Interrupt	WDT_vect
8	0x0E	TIMER2 COMPA	Timer/Counter2 Compare Match A	TIMER2_COMPA_vect
9	0x10	TIMER2 COMPB	Timer/Counter2 Compare Match B	TIMER2_COMPB_vect
10	0x12	TIMER2 OVF	Timer/Counter2 Overflow	TIMER2_OVF_vect
11	0x14	TIMER1 CAPT	Timer/Counter1 Capture Event	TIMER1_CAPT_vect
12	0x16	TIMER1 COMPA	Timer/Counter1 Compare Match A	TIMER1_COMPA_vect
13	0x18	TIMER1 COMPB	Timer/Counter1 Compare Match B	TIMER1_COMPB_vect
14	0x1A	TIMER1 OVF	Timer/Counter1 Overflow	TIMER1_OVF_vect
15	0x1C	TIMER0 COMPA	Timer/Counter0 Compare Match A	TIMER0_COMPA_vect
16	0x1E	TIMER0 COMPB	Timer/Counter0 Compare Match B	TIMER0_COMPB_vect
17	0x20	TIMER0 OVF	Timer/Counter0 Overflow	TIMER0_OVF_vect
18	0x22	SPI, STC	SPI Serial Transfer Complete	SPI_STC_vect
19	0x24	USART, RX	USART Rx Complete	USART_RX_vect
20	0x26	USART, UDRE	USART, Data Register Empty	USART_UDRE_vect
21	0x28	USART, TX	USART, Tx Complete	USART_TX_vect
22	0x2A	ADC	ADC Conversion Complete	ADC_vect
23	0x2C	EE READY	EEPROM Ready	EE_READY_vect
24	0x2E	ANALOG COMP	Analog Comparator	ANALOG_COMP_vect
25	0x30	TWI	2-wire Serial Interface	TWI_vect
26	0x32	SPM READY	Store Program Memory Ready	SPM_READY_vect

Table 1   Interrupt Vector Table ATmega328

4 External Interrupts INT0 & INT1

The interrupts INT0 and INT1 (INTx) are requested at certain levels on pins PD2 and PD3 of the ATmega328 (Arduino Uno: Digital IO 2 and 3).

4.1 Registers for INT0 & INT1

The interrupt behavior is controlled via the register EICRA according to Table 2.

Bit	7	6	5	4	3	2	1	0	
(0x69)	-	-	-	-	ISC11	ISC10	ISC01	ISC00	EICRA
Read/Write	R	R	R	R	R/W	R/W	R/W	R/W	
Initial value	0	0	0	0	0	0	0	0	

ISCx1	ISCx0	Description
0	0	Interrupt request by Lo at INTx (LOW)
0	1	Interrupt request by level change at INTx (CHANGE)
1	0	Interrupt request by falling edge at INTx (FALLING)
1	1	Interrupt request by rising edge at INTx (RISING)

Table 2   Configuration INTx

The interrupt enable bits are located in the EIMSK register - the interrupt flags in the EIFR register.

Bit	7	6	5	4	3	2	1	0	
0x1D (0x3D)	·	·	·	·	·	·	INT1	INT0	EIMSK
Read/Write	R	R	R	R	R	R	R/W	R/W	
Initial value	0	0	0	0	0	0	0	0	

Bit	7	6	5	4	3	2	1	0	
0x1C (0x3C)	·	·	·	·	·	·	INTF1	INTF0	EIFR
Read/Write	R	R	R	R	R	R	R/W	R/W	
Initial value	0	0	0	0	0	0	0	0	

4.2 INTx Program Sample

For the handling of the interrupts INT0 and INT1, the functions `attachInterrupt(interrupt, function, mode)` and `detachInterrupt(interrupt, function, mode)`, which hide the register handling, are already available in the Arduino language.

In the program example *externalInterrupt.ino* (Listing 3) the serial data output is controlled by these two interrupts.

```
// Title      : External Interrupt
// Author     : Claus Kuehnel <ckuehnel@gmx.ch>
// Date       : 2017-05-10
// Id         : externalInterrupt.ino
// Tested w/  : Arduino 1.8.0
//
// DISCLAIMER:
// The author is in no way responsible for any problems
or damage caused by
// using this code. Use at your own risk.
//
// LICENSE:
// This code is distributed under the GNU Public License
// which can be found at
http://www.gnu.org/licenses/gpl.txt
//

const int pLED = 13; // LED at Pin13
const int pINT0 = 2; // INT0 at Pin2
const int pINT1 = 3; // INT1 at Pin3
```

```
volatile boolean iflag = true;

int idx;

void setup()
{
  Serial.begin(19200);
  pinMode(pLED, OUTPUT);

  pinMode(pINT0, INPUT);
  digitalWrite(pINT0, HIGH); // Pullup active

  pinMode(pINT1, INPUT);
  digitalWrite(pINT1, HIGH); // Pullup active

  attachInterrupt(0, stop_serial, FALLING); // INT0 stops
serial output
  Serial.print("EICRA: "); Serial.println(EICRA, HEX);
  attachInterrupt(1, resume_serial, FALLING); // INT1
resumes serial output
  Serial.print("EICRA: "); Serial.println(EICRA, HEX);
  Serial.println("Setup finished.");
}

void loop()
{
  if (iflag) Serial.println(idx);   // iflag controls
serial output
  idx++;
  delay(500);
}

void stop_serial()
{
  iflag = false;
  digitalWrite(pLED, HIGH);
}

void resume_serial()
{
  iflag = true;
  digitalWrite(pLED, LOW);
}
```

Listing 3 Source code *externalInterrupt.ino*

Interrupts INT0 and INT1 are fix assigned to the two inputs PD2 and PD3 of the ATmega328 (Arduino Uno: Digital IO 2 and 3). The corresponding pins are therefore constants.

In the setup routine, these two pins are set as input with pull-up resistor activated. The interrupt INT0 is used to link the routine `stop_serial()`, and INT1 `resume_serial()`. The global interrupt is already enabled by the initialization, so this does not have to be done explicitly.

The EICRA register shows the value 0x0A at the end of the setup, which means that both inputs request a corresponding interrupt for a falling edge.

An index is incremented in the main loop of the program. The output of the index value can be stopped by INT0 and resumed by INT1. The connected LED signals the respective state.

Figure 10 shows the terminal output of the program example. At the beginning, the initialization values of the registers involved are output to the console. At the level of the index value of 1, the output was interrupted. When the output was continued, the index value was already increased to 12.

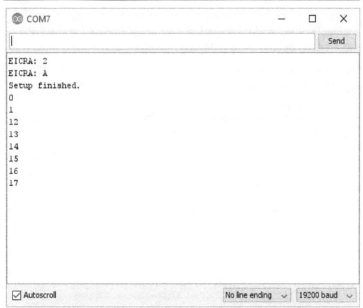

Figure 10   Terminal output *externalInterrupt.ino*

5 Pin Changed Interrupts PCINTx

The interrupts PCIx respond to changes (level changed) of the assigned IO pins. Interrupt PCI2 is assigned to the inputs PCINT23 to PCINT16. Interrupt PCI1 is assigned to the inputs PCINT15 to PCINT8 and the interrupt PCI0 is assigned to PCINT7 to PCINT0.

5.1 Registers for PCINTx

The interrupt behavior is controlled via the PCICR and PCMSKx registers. The bits PCIEx provide for a group-wise Enable according to the above assignment. The individual input can then be enabled in the PCMSKx registers.

ARDUINO

Bit	7	6	5	4	3	2	1	0	
(0x68)	-	-	-	-	-	PCIE2	PCIE1	PCIE0	PCICR
Read/Write	R	R	R	R	R	R/W	R/W	R/W	
Initial value	0	0	0	0	0	0	0	0	

Bit	7	6	5	4	3	2	1	0	
0x1B (0x3B)	-	-	-	-	-	PCIF2	PCIF1	PCIF0	PCIFR
Read/Write	R	R	R	R	R	R/W	R/W	R/W	
Initial value	0	0	0	0	0	0	0	0	

Bit	7	6	5	4	3	2	1	0	
(0x6D)	PCINT23	PCINT22	PCINT21	PCINT20	PCINT19	PCINT18	PCINT17	PCINT16	PCMSK2
Read/Write	R/W	R/W	R/W	R/W	R/W	R/W	R/W	R/W	
Initial value	0	0	0	0	0	0	0	0	

Bit	7	6	5	4	3	2	1	0	
(0x6C)	PCINT15	PCINT14	PCINT13	PCINT12	PCINT11	PCINT10	PCINT9	PCINT8	PCMSK1
Read/Write	R/W	R/W	R/W	R/W	R/W	R/W	R/W	R/W	
Initial value	0	0	0	0	0	0	0	0	

Bit	7	6	5	4	3	2	1	0	
(0x6B)	PCINT7	PCINT6	PCINT5	PCINT4	PCINT3	PCINT2	PCINT1	PCINT0	PCMSK0
Read/Write	R/W	R/W	R/W	R/W	R/W	R/W	R/W	R/W	
Initial value	0	0	0	0	0	0	0	0	

5.2 PCINTx Program Sample

The program example *PCINT.ino* is practically identical to the previous program example. Listing 4 shows the source code of this program.

```
// Title     : PCINT
// Author    : Claus Kuehnel <ckuehnel@gmx.ch>
// Date      : 2017-05-10
// Id        : PCInt.ino
// Tested w/ : Arduino 1.8.0
//
// DISCLAIMER:
// The author is in no way responsible for any problems
or damage caused by
// using this code. Use at your own risk.
//
// LICENSE:
// This code is distributed under the GNU Public License
```

34

```
// which can be found at
http://www.gnu.org/licenses/gpl.txt
//
// Definition of interrupt names
#include <avr/io.h>
// ISR interrupt service routine
#include <avr/interrupt.h>

const int pLED = 13;              // LED at Pin13
const int pPCINT8 = A0;           // PCINT8 at Analog In 0
const int pPCINT9 = A1;           // PCINT9 at Analog In 1

volatile boolean iflag = true;

int idx;

// Install the interrupt routine for PCINT
ISR(PCINT1_vect)
{
  if ( !(PINC & (1<<PINC0)) ) // Detects Change at Analog
In 0
  {
    iflag = false;
    digitalWrite(pLED, HIGH);
  }
  if ( !(PINC & (1<<PINC1)) ) // Detects Change at Analog
In 1
  {
    iflag = true;
    digitalWrite(pLED, LOW);
  }
}

void setup()
{
  Serial.begin(19200);
  pinMode(pLED, OUTPUT);
  digitalWrite(pLED, LOW);

  pinMode(pPCINT8, INPUT);
  digitalWrite(pPCINT8, HIGH); // Pullup active

  pinMode(pPCINT9, INPUT);
  digitalWrite(pPCINT9, HIGH); // Pullup active

  PCICR = 1<<PCIE1; // PCINT8 - PCINT15 enabled
  Serial.print("PCICR: "); Serial.println(PCICR, HEX);
  PCMSK1 |= (1<<PCINT8);    // tell pin change mask to
listen to Analog In 0
  Serial.print("PCMSK1: "); Serial.println(PCMSK1, HEX);
```

35

```
  PCMSK1 |= (1<<PCINT9);      //  tell pin change mask to
listen to Analog In 0
  Serial.print("PCMSK1: "); Serial.println(PCMSK1, HEX);
  sei();
  Serial.println("Setup finished.");
}

void loop()
{
  if (iflag) Serial.println(idx);  // iflag controls
serial output
  idx++;
  delay(500);
}
```

Listing 4   Source code *PCInt.ino*

The inputs PC0 (PCINT8) and PC1 (PCINT9) of ATmega328 (Arduino Uno: Analog In 0 and 1) influence the terminal output of the main loop via the corresponding interrupts.

Both pins are initialized as input with pull-up resistor activated. Both inputs trigger an interrupt request from PCI1, which is why this group must be enabled. In addition, the relevant bits must be set in the interrupt mask.

The interrupt service routine is started in both cases, so the ISR must request the input that requested the interrupt. The iflag and the LED are set accordingly.

In the main loop of the program example, an index is incremented again. The output of the index value can be stopped by PCINT8 and resumed by PCINT9. The connected LED signals the respective state.

Figure 11 shows the terminal outputs of this program example. At the beginning, the initialization values of the registers involved are output to the console. At the level of the index value of 4, output was interrupted. When the output was continued, the index value was already increased to 14.

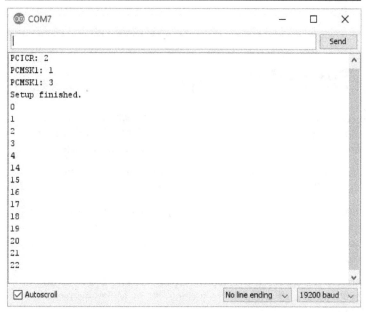

Figure 11   Terminal output *PCINT.ino*

6 Timer Interrupts

The ATmega328 has three timers/counters, which are used in Arduino Uno to generate PWM signals. Timer0 and Timer2 are 8-bit timers/counters. Timer1 is a 16-bit timer/counter.

Timer0 derives various times, e.g. for holding loops, such as `delay()`. Its function is not touched here.

If one can do without PWM in its application, then the other timers/counters can also be used for further purposes. In the following sections, we will use Timer1 and Timer2 for timer interrupts to form a time base.

Table 3 shows the maximum timer period and the resolution for both timers at a clock frequency of 16 MHz, as used in Arduino Uno.

Clock generation by Timer2 at 16 MHz							
Prescaler	1	8	32	64	128	256	1024
Maximum timer period [ms]	0.016	0.128	0.512	1.024	2.048	4.096	16.384
Resolution [ms]	0.063	0.5	2	4	8	16	64
Clock generation by Timer1 at 16 MHz							
Prescaler	1	8	32	64	128	256	1024
Maximum timer period [ms]	4.098	32.784	131.136	262.272	524.544	1049.088	4196.352
Resolution [ms]	0.063	0.5	2	4	8	16	64

Table 3   Clock generation by Timer1 and Timer2

The following function is valid for both timers

$$Count = \frac{f_{CLK} * T}{prescaler}$$

in which the counting range for Timer2 is limited to 0...255 and for Timer1 to 0...65537.

6.1 Registers for Timer2

Timer2 can generate three different interrupts. In the register TIMSK2, the two Output Compare Match interrupts can be enabled via bits OCIE2B and OCIE2A as well as the timer overflow interrupt via bit TOIE2.

Bit	7	6	5	4	3	2	1	0	
(0xB1)	•	•	•	•	•	OCIE2B	OCIE2A	TOIE2	TIMSK2
Read/Write	r	r	R	R	R	R/W	R/W	R/W	
Initial value	0	0	0	0	0	0	0	0	

In the case of the Output Compare Match Interrupt, the interrupt request occur when the timer register TCNT2 has reached the value of the register OCR2A or OCR2B. The timer overflow interrupt is set to 0 when the register is overrun.

The configuration of Timer2 is performed via the registers TCCR2A and TCCR2B according to Table 4 to Table 6.

Bit	7	6	5	4	3	2	1	0	
(0xB0)	COM2A1	COM2A0	COM2B1	COM2B0	•	•	WGM21	WGM20	TCCR2A
Read/Write	R/W	R/W	R/W	R/W	R	R	R/W	R/W	
Initial value	0	0	0	0	0	0	0	0	

Bit	7	6	5	4	3	2	1	0	
(0xB1)	FOC2A	FOC2B	•	•	WGM22	CS22	CS21	CS20	TCCR2B
Read/Write	W	W	R	R	R/W	R/W	R/W	R/W	
Initial value	0	0	0	0	0	0	0	0	

COM2x1	COM2x0	Function
0	0	Normal port function, OC2x disconnected from pin
0	1	Toggle OC2x at Output Compare Match Interrupt
1	0	Reset OC2x at Output Compare Match Interrupt
1	1	Set OC2x at Output Compare Match Interrupt

Table 4   Configuration of output OC2A respectively OC2B

CS22	CS21	CS20	Function
0	0	0	Timer/Counter stopped
0	0	1	Prescaler = 1
0	1	0	Prescaler = 8
0	1	1	Prescaler = 32
1	0	0	Prescaler = 64
1	0	1	Prescaler = 128
1	1	0	Prescaler = 256
1	1	1	Prescaler = 1024

Table 5   Selection of Prescaler

WGM22	WGM21	WGM20	Mode	TOP
0	0	0	Normal Mode	0xFF
0	1	0	CTC Mode	OCR2A

Table 6   Setting the operating mode – excerpt

6.2 Register for Timer1

Timer1 can generate four different interrupts. In the register TIMSK1, the two Output Compare Match interrupts can be enabled via bits OCIE1B and OCIE1A, the timer overflow interrupt via bit TOIE1 and the input capture interrupt via bit ICIE1. The Input Capture Interrupt is not considered here further.

Bit	7	6	5	4	3	2	1	0	
(0x6F)	-	-	ICIE1	-	-	OCIE1B	OCIE1A	TOIE1	TIMSK1
Read/Write	R	R	R/W	R	R	R/W	R/W	R/W	
Initial value	0	0	0	0	0	0	0	0	

In the case of the Output Compare Match Interrupts, the interrupt request is made when the timer register TCNT1 has reached the value of the register OCR1A or OCR1B. The timer overflow interrupt is set to 0 when the register is overflowed from 0xFFFF.

Since Timer1 is a 16-bit timer/counter, the registers OCR1A and OCR1B are 16-bit registers, too.

The configuration of Timer1 is performed via the registers TCCR1A and TCCR1B according to Table 7 to Table 9.

Bit	7	6	5	4	3	2	1	0	
(0x80)	COM1A1	COM1A0	COM1B1	COM1B0	-	-	WGM11	WGM10	TCCR1A
Read/Write	R/W	R/W	R/W	R/W	R	R	R/W	R/W	
Initial value	0	0	0	0	0	0	0	0	

Bit	7	6	5	4	3	2	1	0	
(0x81)	ICNC1	ICES1	-	WGM13	WGM12	CS12	CS11	CS10	TCCR2B
Read/Write	W	W	R	R	R/W	R/W	R/W	R/W	
Initial value	0	0	0	0	0	0	0	0	

COM1x1	COM1x0	Function
0	0	Normal port function, OC1x disconnected from pin
0	1	Toggle OC1x at Output Compare Match Interrupt
1	0	Reset OC1x at Output Compare Match Interrupt
1	1	Set OC1x at Output Compare Match Interrupt

Table 7 Configuration of output OC1A respectively OC1B

CS12	CS11	CS10	Function
0	0	0	Timer/Counter stopped
0	0	1	Prescaler = 1
0	1	0	Prescaler = 8
0	1	1	Prescaler = 64
1	0	0	Prescaler = 256
1	0	1	Prescaler = 1024
1	1	0	External clock at T1 (falling edge)
1	1	1	External clock at T1 (rising edge)

Table 8 Selection of Prescaler or external clock

WGM13	WGM12	WGM11	WGM10	Mode	TOP
0	0	0	0	Normal Mode	0xFFFF
0	1	0	0	CTC Mode	OCR1A

Table 9   Setting the operating mode – excerpt

6.3 Timer2 Program Sample

In the following program example Timer2 should generate a clock of 10 ms.

From Table 3, a prescaler of 1024 can be obtained for Timer2 for a maximum timer period of approx. 16 ms. After 156 clocks the time of 10 ms is reached.

If you run Timer2 in the CTC mode and load the Output Compare Register with a value of 0x9C (= 156), an interrupt request is obtained after 10 ms.

Listing 5 shows the source code of the program example *msecTimer.ino*. In the interrupt service routine, the variable `count` is counted up and register OCR2A is reloaded. The variable count is evaluated in the main loop.

In the setup routine, the initialization of the registers of Timer2 is performed according to the previously described specifications.

In the main loop, the variable `count` is requested. If this value reaches 50 after 500 ms, a character is output at the terminal and the LED is toggled. The flashing of LED with a rate of one second (2 x 500 ms) serves as an indicator of the expected function. Figure 12 shows the terminal output of the program example *msecTimer.ino*.

```
// Title      : msecTimer
// Author     : Claus Kuehnel <ckuehnel@gmx.ch>
// Date       : 2017-05-10
// Id         : msecTimer.ino
// Tested w/  : Arduino 1.8.0
```

```
//
// DISCLAIMER:
// The author is in no way responsible for any problems
or damage caused by
// using this code. Use at your own risk.
//
// LICENSE:
// This code is distributed under the GNU Public License
// which can be found at
http://www.gnu.org/licenses/gpl.txt
//
// Definition of interrupt names
#include <avr/io.h>
// ISR interrupt service routine
#include <avr/interrupt.h>

const int pLED = 13;              // LED at Pin13
volatile byte count;
byte reload = 0x9C; // reload value for 10 ms Timer2
interrupt

// Install the interrupt routine for Timer2 CompareA
ISR(TIMER2_COMPA_vect)
{
  count++;
  OCR2A = reload;
}

void setup()
{
  Serial.begin(19200);
  pinMode(pLED, OUTPUT);
  digitalWrite(pLED, LOW);

  cli();
  TCCR0B = 0;    // stop timer0
  OCR2A = reload;
  Serial.print("OCR2A: "); Serial.println(OCR2A, HEX);
  TCCR2A = 1<<WGM21;
  Serial.print("TCCR2A: "); Serial.println(TCCR2A, HEX);
  TCCR2B = (1<<CS22) | (1<<CS21) | (1<<CS20);
  Serial.print("TCCR2B: "); Serial.println(TCCR2B, HEX);
  TIMSK2 = (1<<OCIE2A);
  Serial.print("TIMSK2: "); Serial.println(TIMSK2, HEX);
  sei();
  Serial.println("Setup finished.");
}

void loop()
{
  if (count == 50)
```

43

```
  {
    flash();
    Serial.print(".");
    count = 0;
  }
}

void flash()
{
  static boolean output = HIGH;

  digitalWrite(pLED, output);
  output = !output;
}
```

Listing 5 Source code _msecTimer.ino_

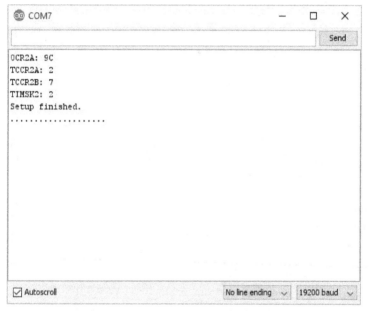

Figure 12 Terminal output _msecTimer.ino_

6.4 Timer1 Program Sample

In the following program example Timer1 should generate a clock of one second.

Table 3 shows a prescaler of 256 for a maximum timer period of approx. 1050 ms. After 62500 cycles the time of 1 s is reached.

If you run Timer1 in the CTC mode and load the output compare register with a value of 0xF424 (= 62500), an interrupt request is obtained after 1 s.

Listing 6 shows the source code for the program sample *secTimer.ino*. In the interrupt service routine, the variable `count` is incremented and the LED is toggled.

In the setup routine, the initialization of the registers of Timer1 is performed according to the previously described specifications.

In the main loop, the output of the variable `count` is carried out every 200 ms. After five outputs of the same value of the variable `count` (5 x 200 ms) the ISR increases its value. The flashing in two-second intervals (2 x 1 s) serves as an indicator of the expected function. Figure 13 shows the terminal output of the program example *secTimer.ino*.

```
// Title      : secTimer
// Author     : Claus Kuehnel <ckuehnel@gmx.ch>
// Date       : 2017-05-10
// Id         : secTimer.ino
// Tested w/  : Arduino 1.8.0
//
// DISCLAIMER:
// The author is in no way responsible for any problems
or damage caused by
// using this code. Use at your own risk.
//
// LICENSE:
// This code is distributed under the GNU Public License
// which can be found at
http://www.gnu.org/licenses/gpl.txt
//
```

```
// Definition of interrupt names
#include <avr/io.h>
// ISR interrupt service routine
#include <avr/interrupt.h>


const int pLED = 13;              // LED at Pin13
unsigned int reload = 0xF424;     // OCR1A Reload for one
second@16 MHz clock & prescaler 256
volatile int count;

// Install the interrupt routine for Timer1 CompareA
ISR(TIMER1_COMPA_vect)
{
  count++;
  flash();
}

void setup()
{
  Serial.begin(19200);
  pinMode(pLED, OUTPUT);
  digitalWrite(pLED, LOW);

  cli();
  TCCR1A = 0;
  TCCR1B = 0;                      // Stop Timer1
  OCR1A = reload;
  TCCR1B = (1<<WGM12) | (1<<CS12);   // CTC Mode
Prescaler = 256
  TIMSK1 = (1<<OCIE1A);         // Timer1 CompareA
Interrupt enable
  sei();                          // Global Interrupt
enable

  Serial.print("OCR1A: "); Serial.println(OCR1A, HEX);
  Serial.print("TCCR1A: "); Serial.println(TCCR1A, HEX);
  Serial.print("TCCR1B: "); Serial.println(TCCR1B, HEX);
  Serial.print("TIMSK1: "); Serial.println(TIMSK1, HEX);
  Serial.println("Setup finished.");
}

void loop()
{
  Serial.println(count);                 // do anything
  delay(200);
}

void flash()
{
  static boolean output = HIGH;
```

```
  digitalWrite(pLED, output);
  output = !output;
}
```

Listing 6 Source code secTimer.ino

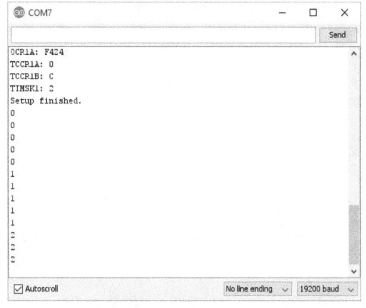

Figure 13 Terminal output secTimer.ino

7 Watchdog

A watchdog prevents the total failure of a microcontroller after a program crash by a system reset or calling another function.

The application software must reset the watchdog running as a timer before a certain time has elapsed. If it is not capable of doing so, the function assigned to the watchdog is triggered.

The watchdog in an ATmega328 can trigger a reset as well as a watchdog interrupt. It is precisely through the latter possibility that the watchdog can also exercise other functions, such as those of a system timer.

The watchdog is clocked by a separate on-chip oscillator. A prescaler can be used to set time-outs from 16 ms to 8 s. The clock frequency generated by the on-chip oscillator depends from temperature and operating voltage, so that the expectations of their constancy have to be kept within limits. The watchdog is therefore less suitable for timely precise tasks.

Figure 14 shows the block diagram of the watchdog in the ATmega328 and the relevant settings.

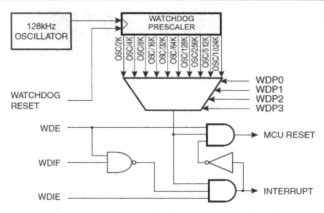

Figure 14   Watchdog block diagram

7.1 Watchdog Register

The watchdog is controlled by the WDTCSR register. The bits WDP3-WDP0 determine the time-out according to Table 10. The watchdog is configured according to Table 11.

Bit	7	6	5	4	3	2	1	0	
(0x60)	WDIF	WDIE	WDP3	WDCE	WDE	WDP2	WDP11	WDP0	WDTCSR
Read/Write	R	R/W	R/W	R/W	R/W	R/W	R/W	R/W	
Initial value	0	0	0	0	0	0	0	0	

WDP3	WDP2	WDP1	WDP0	Watchdog Oscillator Cycles	Time-Out
0	0	0	0	2 K	16 ms
0	0	0	1	4 K	32 ms
0	0	1	0	8 K	64 ms
0	0	1	1	16 K	0.125 s
0	1	0	0	32 K	0.250 s
0	1	0	1	64 K	0.5 s
0	1	1	0	128 K	1 s
0	1	1	1	256 K	2 s
1	0	0	0	512 K	4 s
1	0	0	1	1024 K	8 s

Table 10   Watchdog Time-Out Periods

WDTON Fuse	WDE	WDIE	Mode	Action
1	0	0	Stop	no
1	0	1	Interrupt	Interrupt
1	1	0	System Reset	System Reset
1	1	1	Interrupt & System Reset	Interrupt -> System Reset
0	x	x	System Reset	System Reset

Table 11   Watchdog Configuration

7.2 Watchdog Interrupt Program Sample

In the program example*d.ino* (Listing 24), the watchdog triggers an interrupt that toggles the connected LED. The watchdog reset, which must be executed by the program before the set watchdog period has elapsed, is defined by the macro `wdt_reset()` as an inline assembler statement. In the setup routine, the watchdog register WDTCSR is initialized in such a way that a watchdog period of approx. 1 s is obtained.

In the main loop, only an index is incremented and output before a waiting time (`delay (1500)`) is executed. Since no watchdog reset can occur during this watchdog period, the corresponding interrupt causes the LED to toggle.

If this time is reduced to a value less than 1 s (for example, `delay (500)`), the watchdog is reset before the watchdog period expires, and the LED remains unchanged. Figure 15 shows the terminal outputs of the *watchdog.ino* program example.

```
// Title      : Watchdog
// Author     : Claus Kuehnel <ckuehnel@gmx.ch>
// Date       : 2017-05-10
// Id         : watchdog.ino
// Tested w/  : Arduino 1.8.0
//
// DISCLAIMER:
// The author is in no way responsible for any problems
or damage caused by
// using this code. Use at your own risk.
//
// LICENSE:
// This code is distributed under the GNU Public License
// which can be found at
http://www.gnu.org/licenses/gpl.txt
//
// Definition of interrupt names
#include <avr/io.h>
// ISR interrupt service routine
#include <avr/interrupt.h>

#define wdt_reset()  __asm__ __volatile__ ("wdr")

const int pLED = 13; // LED at Pin13

int idx;

// Install the interrupt routine for Watchdog Interrupt
ISR(WDT_vect)
{
  flash();
}

void setup()
{
  Serial.begin(19200);
  pinMode(pLED, OUTPUT);
  digitalWrite(pLED, LOW);

  cli();
  wdt_reset();
  WDTCSR |= (1<<WDCE) | (1<<WDE); // Start timed sequence
```

```
  WDTCSR = (1<<WDIE) | (1<<WDP2) | (1<<WDP1); // Set new
prescaler = 128K cycles (~1 s)
  sei();

  Serial.print("WDTCSR: ");
  Serial.println(WDTCSR, HEX);
  Serial.println("Setup finished.");
}

void loop()
{
  Serial.println(idx++); // do anything
  delay(1500); // change argument to 1500 -> watchdog
will be active
  wdt_reset();
}

void flash()
{
  static boolean output = HIGH;

  digitalWrite(pLED, output);
  output = !output;
}
```

Listing 7   Source code *watchdog.ino*

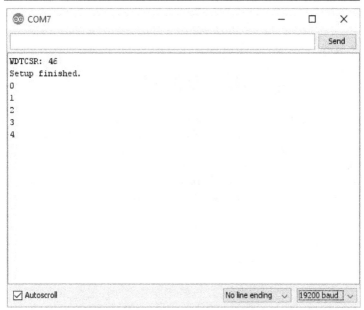

Figure 15   Terminal output *watchdog.ino*

8 Analog Comparator

The Analog Comparator compares the voltage values at pins PD6 and PD7 (Arduino Uno: Digital IO 6 and 7). If the voltage at PD6 is higher than at PD7, then the output of the comparator is set. This output can be used to request an interrupt. Figure 16 shows a block diagram of the analog comparator and the circuit parts surrounding it.

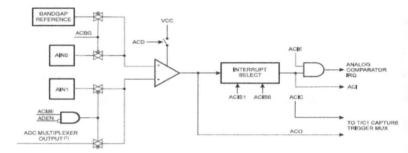

Figure 16 Block diagram Analog Comparator

8.1 Registers for Analog Comparator

The control of the analog comparator is essentially provided by the register ACSR. If the bit ACME in register ADCSRB is reset, then AIN1 is switched to the comparator (A-). The same is true when ACME is set in ADCSRB and ADEN in ACSRA (see ADC). If ACME is set and ADEN is reset, then an ADC channel is switched to the comparator, depending on the assignment of the MUX bits.

Bit	7	6	5	4	3	2	1	0	
(0x7B)	-	ACME	-	-	-	ADTS2	ADTS1	ADTS0	ADCSRB
Read/Write	R	R/W	R	R	R	R/W	R/W	R/W	
Initial value	0	0	0	0	0	0	0	0	

Bit	7	6	5	4	3	2	1	0	
0x30 (0x50)	ACD	ACBG	ACO	ACI	ACIE	ACIC	ACIS1	ACIS0	ACSR
Read/Write	R/W	R/W	R	R/W	R/W	R/W	R/W	R/W	
Initial value	0	0	n/a	0	0	0	0	0	

The comparator can be switched off via bit ACD and the bandgap reference can be connected to the comparator (A +) with ACBG. The bits ACIE and ACIC enable the interrupt or the input capture. The interrupt configuration takes place via the bits ACIS1 and ACIS0 according to Table 12.

ACIS1	ACIS0	Interrupt Mode
0	0	Comparator Interrupt at level change on ACO
0	1	reserved
1	0	Comparator Interrupt at falling edge on ACO
1	1	Comparator Interrupt at rising edge on ACO

Table 12   Comparator Interrupt Configuration

8.2 Analog Comparator Program Sample

In the program example *acomp.ino* (Listing 8), the analog comparator triggers an interrupt which, depending on the status of the comparator output ACO, sets the flag `iflag` and turns the connected LED on or off.

In the setup routine, the analog comparator is initialized so that the bandgap reference is present at input A+ and input A- is connected to AIN1.

In the main loop of the program example, an index is incremented again. The output of the index value can be stopped or resumed by the level at pin AIN1. The connected LED signals the respective state.

Figure 17 shows the terminal outputs of the program example. Initially, the initialization of the registers involved is output. At the level of the index value of 4, output was interrupted. When the output was continued, the index value had already been increased to 12.

```
// Title      : ACOMP
// Author     : Claus Kuehnel <ckuehnel@gmx.ch>
// Date       : 2017-05-10
// Id         : acomp.ino
// Tested w/   : Arduino 1.8.0
//
// DISCLAIMER:
// The author is in no way responsible for any problems
or damage caused by
// using this code. Use at your own risk.
//
// LICENSE:
// This code is distributed under the GNU Public License
// which can be found at
http://www.gnu.org/licenses/gpl.txt
//
// Definition of interrupt names
#include <avr/io.h>
// ISR interrupt service routine
#include <avr/interrupt.h>

const int pLED = 13;                 // LED at Pin13
const int pAIN1 = 7;                 // AIN1 at Pin7

volatile boolean iflag = true;

int idx;

// Install the interrupt routine for ACOMP
ISR(ANALOG_COMP_vect)
{
  if ( ACSR & (1<<ACO) )        // ACO is set?
  {
    iflag = false;
    digitalWrite(pLED, HIGH);
  }
  else
  {
    iflag = true;
    digitalWrite(pLED, LOW);
  }
}

void setup()
```

```
{
  Serial.begin(19200);
  pinMode(pLED, OUTPUT);
  digitalWrite(pLED, LOW);

  pinMode(pAIN1, INPUT);

  cli();
  ADCSRA &= ~(1<<ADEN);                 // ADC disabled
  ADCSRB |= ~(1<<ACME);                 // AMUX enabled
  ACSR = (1<<ACBG) | (1<<ACIE);         // ACOMP Interrupt
enabled
  DIDR1 = (1<<AIN1D) | (1<< AIN0D);
  sei();

  Serial.print("ADCSRA: "); Serial.println(ADCSRA, HEX);
  Serial.print("ADCSRB: "); Serial.println(ADCSRB, HEX);
  Serial.print("ACSR: "); Serial.println(ACSR, HEX);
  Serial.print("DIDR1: "); Serial.println(DIDR1, HEX);
  Serial.println("Setup finished.");
}

void loop()
{
  if (iflag) Serial.println(idx);  // iflag controls
serial output
  idx++;
  delay(500);
}
```

Listing 8   Source code *acomp.ino*

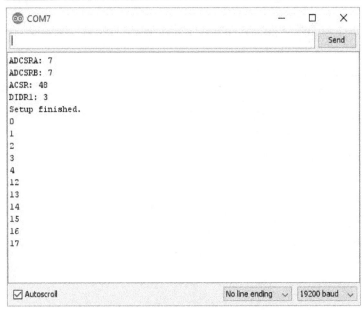

Figure 17   Terminal output *acomp.ino*

9 Analog/Digital-Converter

The ATmega328 has an ADC with 10-bit resolution operating according to the method of successive approximation.

The analog input voltage is compared with the output voltage of a DAC. The output voltage of the DAC is determined by the control logic as well as one of the reference voltages. The control logic controls the DAC bit by bit and the output signal of the comparator determines whether the respective bit is set or reset in the output register. In this way, the output voltage of the DA converter successively approaches the analog voltage value to be detected.

This voltage value must not change during the conversion process since this would lead to a faulty content of the output register. A sample and hold circuit before the comparator satisfies this requirement.

The required conversion time is independent of the applied input voltage and depends only on the resolution of the ADC. A 10-bit ADC requires exactly ten conversion steps, the time of which is determined by the clocking of the DAC and the switching time of the comparator.

The input voltage is fed to the comparator via two multiplexers. For calibration, the internal bandgap reference voltage and the ground potential can additionally be fed to the comparator.

An internal reference voltage of 1.1 V or the analog operating voltage AVCC can be used as the analog reference voltage. The input voltage range is between 0 V (GND) and the reference voltage (-1 LSB).

Figure 18 shows a section of the block diagram of the AD converter.

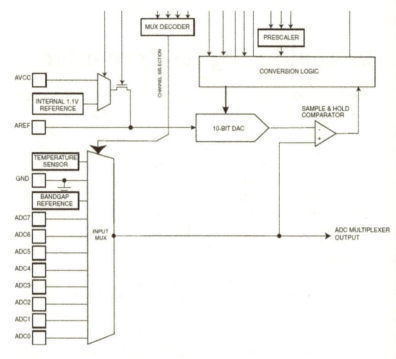

Figure 18   ADC Block diagram

9.1   Registers for ADC

The registers ADMUX, ADCSRA and ADCSRB are responsible for controlling the AD conversion. The result of the AD conversion is saved in the registers ADCH and ADCL.

Bit	7	6	5	4	3	2	1	0	
(0x7C)	REFS1	REFS0	ADLAR	-	MUX3	MUX2	MUX1	MUX0	ADMUX
Read/Write	R/W	R/W	R	R	R/W	R/W	R/W	R/W	
Initial value	0	0	0	0	0	0	0	0	

The bits REFS1 and REFS0 set the reference voltage. After a reset, an external reference voltage is expected at the AVREF connector. Table 13 shows the options selectable.

REFS1	REFS0	Reference Voltage
0	0	AREF, Internal Reference Voltage disconnected
0	1	AVCC with external capacity at pin AREF
1	0	reserved
1	1	Internal 1.1 V reference voltage with external capacity at pin AREF

Table 13 Selection of Reference Voltage

The ADLAR bit specifies whether the result of the AD conversion is left-aligned (ADLAR = 1, xxxxxxxxxx000000) or right-aligned (ADLAR = 0, 000000xxxxxxxxxx) in the 16-bit result.

The MUX3:0 bits program the analog multiplexer. After reset, input ADC0 is active. Table 14 shows the options selectable.

MUX3:0	Input to GND
0000	ADC0
0001	ADC1
0010	ADC2
0011	ADC3
0100	ADC4
0101	ADC5
0110	ADC6
0111	ADC7
1000	Temperature Sensor
1110	Bandgap-Reference 1.1 V
1111	GND 0 V

Table 14 Selection Input Channel

Bit	7	6	5	4	3	2	1	0	
(0x7A)	ADEN	ADSC	ADATE	ADIF	ADIE	ADPS2	ADPS1	ADPS0	ADCSRA
Read/Write	R/W	R/W	R	R/W	R/W	R/W	R/W	R/W	
Initial value	0	0	0	0	0	0	0	0	

The ADEN bit enables the ADC. An AD conversion is started by setting bit ADSC. The bit remains set during the conversion and is deleted by the hardware after the end of the conversion.

The ADATE bit enables the auto-trigger function to be set in the ADCSRB register. ADIF is the AD interrupt flag and ADIE is the AD interrupt enable bit.

The clock frequency of the successive approximation is derived from the oscillator frequency and is determined by a prescaler which is set via the bits ADPS2:0 (Table 15). In order to achieve the maximum resolution, a frequency between 50 kHz and 200 kHz is optimal.

ADSP2	ADSP1	ADSP0	Prescaler
0	0	0	1
0	0	1	2
0	1	0	4
0	1	1	8
1	0	0	16
1	0	1	32
1	1	0	64
1	1	1	128

Table 15 Prescaler Selection for AD conversion

Bit	7	6	5	4	3	2	1	0	
(0x7B)	-	ACME	-	-	-	ADTS2	ADTS1	ADTS0	ADCSRB
Read/Write	R	R/W	R	R	R	R/W	R/W	R/W	
Initial value	0	0	0	0	0	0	0	0	

The bits ADTS2: 0 determine the trigger source for the AD conversion, if the bit ADATE is set in the register ADCSR. Otherwise, they are not affected (Table 16).

ADTS2	ADTS1	ADTS0	Trigger
0	0	0	Free Running Mode
0	0	1	Analog Comparator
0	1	0	External Interrupt INT0
0	1	1	Timer/Counter0 Compare Match A
1	0	0	Timer/Counter0 Overflow
1	0	1	Timer/Counter1 Compare Match B
1	1	0	Timer/Counter1 Overflow
1	1	1	Timer/Counter1 Capture Event

Table 16   Selection of Trigger Source for Auto-trigger

9.2 ADC Program Samples

As the register description has shown, the AD converter of the ATmega328 allows different operating modes and different reference voltages. In addition, the various analog inputs can be routed through the analog multiplexer to the AD converter.

For testing the different operating modes, I always used the internal bandgap reference as the input voltage. In this way one knows the expected result and can concentrate on configuration and initialization.

9.2.1 Software-triggered AD-Conversion

For Arduino the software-triggered AD conversion provides the instruction `analogRead(analogPin)`.

By initialization, the AD converter is already enabled and the prescaler is set to 128. The clock frequency for the AD conversion is 125 kHz at an oscillator frequency of 16 MHz. After 80 µs, an AD conversion is completed. The voltage AVCC serves as a reference voltage.

Since we are dealing with the interrupt modes, this type of AD conversion is not considered further below.

A detailed description of this AD conversion mode is available at http://arduino.cc/en/Reference/AnalogRead.

9.2.2 Free-Running AD-Conversion

In Free Running Mode, the next AD conversion is automatically started after the completion of preceding AD conversion.

Now we want to configure the ADC for the Free Running Mode to measure the bandgap reference voltage.

The reference voltage and the input channel are selected via the ADMUX register. The bits ADEN, ADATE and ADIE of the ADCSRA register are set, which defines an interrupt-controlled auto-trigger function. The desired interrupt source is selected with the bits ADTSx in register ADCSRB.

For the Free Running Mode, the default values after reset (ADTS2:0 = 000) are valid, which is why you do not have to worry about this anymore. The interrupt source is the Interrupt ADC Conversion Complete, which is signaled by the ADIF interrupt flag.

A first result is available in the ADCH and ADCL registers with the start of the second AD conversion. The second and each further AD conversion are started by the interrupt request (ADIF) at the end of the previous AD conversion. Only the first AD conversion is to be started as before by setting the bit ADS.

Listing 9 shows the source code for the program example *adc2s.ino*.

```
// Title       : ADC2s
// Author      : Claus Kuehnel <ckuehnel@gmx.ch>
// Date        : 2017-05-10
// Id          : ADC2s.ino
// Tested w/   : Arduino 1.8.0
//
// DISCLAIMER:
// The author is in no way responsible for any problems
or damage caused by
// using this code. Use at your own risk.
//
```

```
// LICENSE:
// This code is distributed under the GNU Public License
// which can be found at
http://www.gnu.org/licenses/gpl.txt
//
// Definition of interrupt names
#include <avr/io.h>
// ISR interrupt service routine
#include <avr/interrupt.h>

#define ADC0 0
#define TEMP 0b1000
#define VBG  0b1110

const int pLED = 13;            // LED at Pin13
const float VACC = 5.12;        // measured on my Arduino

volatile unsigned int ADC_result;
float voltage;

ISR(ADC_vect)
{
  ADC_result = ADC;
}

void setup()
{
  Serial.begin(19200);
  pinMode(pLED, OUTPUT);
  digitalWrite(pLED, LOW);

  cli();
  ADMUX = (0<<REFS1) | (1<<REFS0);      // AVCC is
reference
  ADMUX |= VBG;                         // VBG selected
  ADCSRA |= (1<<ADEN) | (1<<ADATE) | (1<<ADIE);    // ADC
enabled, prescaler unchanged
  ADCSRB = 0;                           // Free Running
Mode
  ADCSRA |= (1<<ADSC);
  sei();

  Serial.println("ADC Configuration for Free Running
Mode");
  Serial.print("ADMUX: "); Serial.println(ADMUX, HEX);
  Serial.print("ADCSRA: "); Serial.println(ADCSRA, HEX);
  Serial.print("ADCSRB: "); Serial.println(ADCSRB, HEX);
  Serial.print("DIDR0: "); Serial.println(DIDR0, HEX);
  delay(1000);
  Serial.println("ADC free running...");
}
```

65

```
void loop()
{
  cli();
  ADC_result = ADC;
  sei();
  Serial.print("ADC: "); Serial.print(ADC_result,HEX);
  voltage = ADC_result* VACC/1024;
  Serial.print("\tVoltage: "); Serial.print(voltage,3);
  Serial.println(" V");
  delay(1000);
}
```

Listing 9   Source code *ADC2s.ino*

Since the AD conversion is continued continuously in the Free Running Mode, the ISR only provides for the storage of the results of the AD conversion in the variable `ADC_result`.

The AD converter is initialized by directly describing the registers ADMUX, ADCSRA and ADCSRB in the setup routine. The first AD conversion is started by setting the ADSC bit at the end of the initialization.

In the main loop, the result of the last AD conversion is finally determined by querying the variable `ADC_result` and outputted as a hexadecimal number and a calculated voltage value via the serial interface once per second. Figure 19 shows the terminal outputs of the *ADC2s.ino* program.

ARDUINO

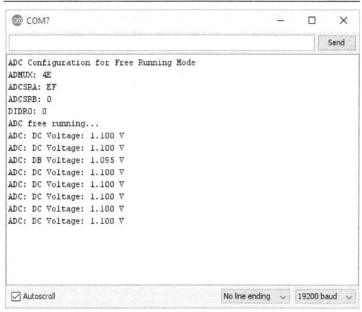

Figure 19   Terminal output *ADC2s.ino*

9.2.3   Timer-controlled AD-Conversion

In many applications of data acquisition, fix timing for acquiring measuring data is required. With the auto-trigger function of the AD-converter considered here, all possibilities are given.

In the following program example, the AD converter is intended to record measured values with a period ofexactly one second.

In order to generate the required clock, the 16-bit timer1 must be used. The counting range of Timer2 comprises only 8 bits and is thus not sufficient. According to Table 3, the timer/counter1 overflow can serve as a trigger event.

The one-second clock signal should therefore trigger the AD converter. The readout of the results is possible after the end of the conversion. Here the ADC interrupt is used to set a flag which is evaluated in the main loop. If a new result of an AD conversion is present, it is read and output via the serial interface.

Otherwise, with a period of 100 ms points are output in the cycle to characterize the activity between the conversions. Figure 20 shows the output of the program *adc3s.ino*.

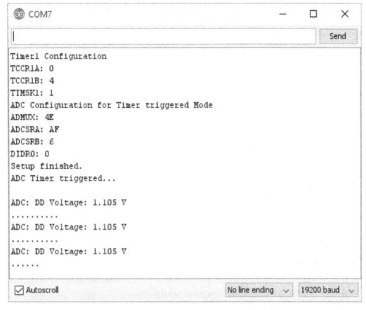

Figure 20   Terminal output *ADC3s.ino*

The program *ADC3s.ino* is comparable to the program *ADC2s.ino*, except that two interrupts (Timer1 Overflow, ADC) are used here. Listing 27 shows the source code of the program example *ADC3s.ino*.

```
// Title      : ADC3s
// Author     : Claus Kuehnel <ckuehnel@gmx.ch>
// Date       : 2017-05-10
```

```
// Id        : ADC3s.ino
// Tested w/  : Arduino 1.8.0
//
// DISCLAIMER:
// The author is in no way responsible for any problems
or damage caused by
// using this code. Use at your own risk.
//
// LICENSE:
// This code is distributed under the GNU Public License
// which can be found at
http://www.gnu.org/licenses/gpl.txt
//
// Definition of interrupt names
#include <avr/io.h>
// ISR interrupt service routine
#include <avr/interrupt.h>

#define ADC0 0
#define TEMP 0b1000
#define VBG  0b1110

const int pLED = 13;              // LED at Pin13
const float VACC = 5.12;          // measured on my
Arduino

unsigned int reload = 0xFFFF - 0xF424; // TCNT1 Reload
for one second@16 MHz clock & prescaler 256
volatile unsigned int ADC_result;
volatile boolean ADC_flag = false;
float voltage;

// Install the interrupt routine for Timer1 Overflow
ISR(TIMER1_OVF_vect)
{
  TCNT1 = reload;
}

// Install the interrupt routine for ADC Interrupt
ISR(ADC_vect)
{
  ADC_flag = true;
  flash();
}

void setup()
{
  Serial.begin(19200);
  pinMode(pLED, OUTPUT);
  digitalWrite(pLED, LOW);
```

69

```
  cli();
  TCCR1A = 0;
  TCCR1B = 0;                          // Stop Timer1
  TCNT1 = reload;
  TCCR1B = (1<<CS12);                  // Normal Mode,
Prescaler = 256
  TIMSK1 = (1<<TOIE1);                 // Timer1 Overflow
Interrupt enable

  ADMUX = (0<<REFS1) | (1<<REFS0);  // AVCC is reference
  ADMUX |= VBG;                        // VBG selected
  ADCSRA |= (1<<ADEN) | (1<<ADATE) | (1<<ADIE);   // ADC
enabled, prescaler unchanged
  ADCSRB = (1<<ADTS2) | (1<< ADTS1);                      //
Triggered by Timer/Counter1 Overflow
  ADCSRA |= (1<<ADSC);
  sei();

  Serial.println("Timer1 Configuration");
  Serial.print("TCCR1A: "); Serial.println(TCCR1A, HEX);
  Serial.print("TCCR1B: "); Serial.println(TCCR1B, HEX);
  Serial.print("TIMSK1: "); Serial.println(TIMSK1, HEX);

  Serial.println("ADC Configuration for Timer triggered
Mode");
  Serial.print("ADMUX: "); Serial.println(ADMUX, HEX);
  Serial.print("ADCSRA: "); Serial.println(ADCSRA, HEX);
  Serial.print("ADCSRB: "); Serial.println(ADCSRB, HEX);
  Serial.print("DIDR0: "); Serial.println(DIDR0, HEX);
  Serial.println("Setup finished.");
  delay(1000);
  Serial.println("ADC Timer triggered...");
}

void loop()
{
  if (ADC_flag)
  {
    cli();
    ADC_result = ADC;
    sei();
    Serial.println();
    Serial.print("ADC: "); Serial.print(ADC_result,HEX);
    voltage = ADC_result* VACC/1024;
    Serial.print("\tVoltage: "); Serial.print(voltage,3);
Serial.println(" V");
    ADC_flag = false;
  }
  else
  {
    Serial.print(".");
```

```
   delay(100);
  }
}

void flash()
{
  static boolean output = HIGH;

  digitalWrite(pLED, output);
  output = !output;
}
```

Listing 10   Source code *ADC3s.ino*

To trigger the AD conversion, the Timer1 Overflow Interrupt is used here. For the overflow to occur exactly after one second, the register TCNT1 is preloaded with the value 0x0BDB (= 0xFFFF - 0xF424). The overflow then occurs after 0xF424 clocks. In the timer ISR, only the reloading of the reload value for the next cycle is performed.

The ADC interrupt only sets the `ADC_flag` and toggles the connected LED.

The initialization of the registers of the AD converter differs only with respect to the selected auto-trigger interrupt source.

The configuration of Timer1 is completely conventional, except that the register TCNT1 is pre-loaded with the reload value.

After enabling the interrupts, the first AD conversion can be started and the program enters the main loop. In this main loop, the `ADC_flag` set in the ADC ISR is interrogated to either read out a new result of an AD conversion, formatted via the serial interface and reset the flag, or a "." and then wait 10 ms.

10 Resume

In this small book I tried to look behind the scenes of the Arduino environment. Various program examples with interrupts have shown how the resources of the microcontroller used can also be accessed at register level.

At the beginning, the terminal outputs always show the value of the configuration registers which are read back after the initialization. This makes it easier to trace the various initialization steps. In a real application program you will certainly do without it.

11 Impressum

Dr. Claus Kühnel

Skript Verlag Kühnel

Talstrasse 13B

CH-8852 Altendorf

eMail: ckuehnel@gmx.ch

Website: www.ckuehnel.ch

www.ingramcontent.com/pod-product-compliance
Lightning Source LLC
Chambersburg PA
CBHW031229050326
40689CB00009B/1529